Nita Mehta's
Oats Breakfast Cookbook

A fresh approach to a healthier oat meal breakfast

Nita Mehta
B.Sc. (Home Science), M.Sc. (Food and Nutrition), Gold Medalist

Nita Mehta's
Oats Breakfast Cookbook
A fresh approach to a healthier oat meal breakfast

© Copyright 2006  Publishers Pvt Ltd

WORLD RIGHTS RESERVED: The contents - all recipes, photographs and drawings are original and copyrighted. No portion of this book shall be reproduced, stored in a retrieval system or transmitted by any means, electronic, mechanical, photocopying, recording or otherwise, without the written permission of the publishers.

While every precaution is taken in the preparation of this book, the publishers and the author assume no responsibility for errors or omissions. Neither is any liability assumed for damages resulting from the use of information contained herein.

TRADEMARKS ACKNOWLEDGED: Trademarks used, if any, are acknowledged as trademarks of their respective owners. These are used as reference only and no trademark infringement is intended upon. Ajinomoto (monosodium glutamade, MSG) is a trademark of Aji-no-moto company of Japan. Use it sparingly if you must as a flavour enhancer.

First Edition 2006

ISBN 81-7869-109-4

Food Styling & Photography: Tanya Mehta

Layout and laser typesetting:

National Information Technology Academy
3A/3, Asaf Ali Road
New Delhi-110002
☎ 23252948

Published by:

Publishers Pvt. Ltd.
3A/3 Asaf Ali Road,
New Delhi - 110002
Tel: 23252948, 23250091
Telefax: 91-11-23250091

Editorial and Marketing office:
E-159, Greater Kailash-II, N.Delhi-48
Fax: 91-11-29225218, 29229558
Tel: 91-11-29214011, 29218727, 29218574
E-Mail: nitamehta@email.com, nitamehta@nitamehta.com
Website: http://www.nitamehta.com
Website: http://www.snabindia.com

Printed at:

BRIJBASI ART PRESS LTD

Price: Rs. 150/-

Foreword

Start your day with oats* – the healthy whole grain cereal. It can be used in a variety of ways. Most of us generally consume this cholesterol lowering magic cereal as oat* porridge only. Here I present a huge innovative collection of specially created oat recipes all thoroughly tried and tested in our kitchen laboratory. We have used it instead of the regular flour (maida) in pancakes and breads. Healthy cakes and cookies of oats* have been carefully created. The South Indian oat* vadas and oat* idlis are a healthy treat.

WHY ARE OATS HEALTHY?

Oats* are low-fat complex carbohydrates with a special soluble fiber called 'beta-glucan'. Oats* has one of the highest concentrations of protein, calcium, iron, magnesium, zinc, copper, manganese, thiamin, folacin and vitamin E; more then other unfortified whole grains, such as wheat, corn, rice and rye.

The soluble fiber in oats* lowers cholesterol. It also helps maintain blood pressure. It can help keep your arteries clean and healthy.

The ability of oat* soluble fibers to absorb water and swell, creates a feeling of fullness and helps in maintaining weight. It also assists people with diabetes in managing their blood sugar levels.

Enjoy cooking these truly healthy recipes with the magic of oats*!

Nita Mehta

Nita Mehta

* For best results, Nita Mehta recommends Quaker Oats.

Contents

Foreword   3

Indian   5

Steamed Oat Surprise   6
Savoury Oat Dalia   8
Masala Oat Pancakes   10
Oats Chaat   12
Oat-Moong Toast   14
Oat Hearts   16
Hari Chutney   18
Mithi Saunth   18

South Indian   19

Oat Pea Dosa   20
Corn Oat Upma   22
Crunchy Oat Poha   24
Mini Vegetable Oat Oothapam   26
Oat Vada   28
Dakshini Toast with Oats   30
Oat Idli   32
Oat Coconut Chutney   34

Continental   35

Oat Patty Sandwiches   36
Spanish Oat Omelette   38
Oat Mushroom Croquettes   40
Fruit Medley Topped with Crunchy Oats   42
Oat Pretzels   44
Quick Oat Sandwiches   46
Sesame Spinach Oat Toasts   48
Oat Club Sandwiches   50
Oat Potato Shells   52
Mayonnaise (Eggless)   54
Chocolate Sauce   54

Sweet Delights   55

Oat Ka Halwa   56
Oat Fudge Fingers   58
Oat Coated Apples   60
Banana/Mango Oat Pancakes   62
Apple Oat Cake   64

Indian

Steamed Oat Surprise

This light snack is quick to make. It is similar to a Gujarati dhokla.

Serves 4-5   Cooking Time: 15 Minutes

INGREDIENTS

1 cup oats*
½ cup semolina (sooji) - roasted
1¼ tsp salt
2½ cups curd, approx.
1 tsp oregano
¼ tsp haldi (optional)
2 tsp eno fruit salt
1 carrot (gajar) - grated
¼ cup chopped capsicum
¼ cup hari chutney

METHOD

1. Roast sooji and oats* separately in a kadhai for 4-5 minutes, stirring continuously. Cool. Mix together.

2. Add salt, curd, oregano and haldi in the sooji and oat mixture to get a light yellow colour. Mix well to get a thick batter.

3. Boil 2 glasses of water in a deep pan (patila). Mix eno with sooji and oats* batter and transfer half of the batter to a greased thali to get ½" thick layer.

4. Sprinkle most of the grated carrot & chopped capsicum over it, keeping aside some for the top. Then sprinkle drops of hari chutney with a spoon all over.

5. Pour the rest of sooji and oats* mixture.

6. Top with the remaining grated carrot and capsicum.

7. Steam for 15-20 minutes. Check with a knife in the centre. If it comes out clean it is done. Cut into 2" triangles or square pieces and again sprinkle grated carrot over it. Top with hari chutney. Serve.

* For best results, Nita Mehta recommends Quaker Oats.

Savoury Oat Dalia

No more sweet dalia, the usual porridge for you! Oats* combined with whole wheat to make an unusual savoury breakfast.

Serves 2   Cooking Time: 4-5 Minutes

INGREDIENTS

¼ cup dalia (cracked wheat) - soaked in water for at least 1 hour or more
½ cup oats*
¼ cup shelled peas (matar) - boiled
1 green chilli - deseeded & chopped
1 small potato - peeled & cut into small pieces
2 tbsp oil, ½ tsp jeera
¼ tsp black pepper - crushed
1 tsp finely chopped ginger
1 tej patta (bay leaf)
1 chhoti illaichi (green cardamom) - crushed
¼ tsp haldi (turmeric powder)
¼ tsp red chilli powder
1 tsp salt
1½ tsp lemon juice, 2 tbsp chopped coriander
¼ tsp garam masala

METHOD

1. Wash and soak dalia in enough water for about an hour or more.

2. Heat 2 tbsp oil in a non stick kadhai or a pan. Add ½ tsp jeera. Let it turn golden.

3. Add crushed black pepper, ginger, tej patta and illaichi together. Reduce flame.

4. Add haldi, salt and red chilli powder. Mix.

5. Add oats*.

6. Add potatoes and stir fry for 1 minute.

7. Add peas & green chilli. Bhuno the vegetables for 1 minute on low flame.

8. Drain the dalia through a fine strainer and add to the vegetables. Stir fry for 2 minutes. Add ½ cup water and mix.

9. Cover tightly & cook further for 2-3 minutes, stirring occasionally. Cook till potatoes turn soft.

10. Remove from fire. Mix in the lemon juice, coriander and garam masala. Serve hot.

Note: Cook dalia in a non stick utensil, otherwise it sticks to the bottom of the utensil while cooking.

* For best results, Nita Mehta recommends Quaker Oats.

Masala Oat Pancakes

A protein rich breakfast of oat flour pancakes. Serve it with hari chutney. The hari chutney can be made a couple of days in advance and refrigerated.

Makes 2-3   Cooking Time: 2-3 Minutes

INGREDIENTS

BATTER
1 cup oats* - ground to a powder in a mixer
1½ cups water, approx.
1 tsp kasoori methi (dry fenugreek leaves)
1 small onion - very finely chopped
1 small tomato - very finely chopped
1 green chilli - deseeded & very finely chopped
1 tbsp chopped coriander
½ tsp red chilli powder, ¾ tsp salt
½ tsp garam masala, ¼ tsp haldi

METHOD

1. Mix all ingredients of the batter together in a bowl. Beat well, adding enough water to make a batter of pouring consistency.

2. Heat a non stick pan (not too hot). Smear 1 tsp oil in the centre.

3. Remove from fire and pour 1½ karchhis of batter. Spread by tilting the pan. If there is any extra batter, just tilt the pan into the bowl of batter to get rid of that extra batter. This way you get a thin pancake.

4. Return to fire. After 1 minute, when the edges get slightly brown, add 1 tsp of oil on the sides.

5. When the top is cooked, add a few drops of oil on the top of the pancake.

6. Turn over when the underside is done. Cook the other side.

7. Fold into half. Serve immediately with tomato ketchup or mint chutney.

* For best results, Nita Mehta recommends Quaker Oats.

Oats Chaat

Stir up this innovative chaat anytime in the evening and your family will love it. But remember to make it fresh and serve it immediately.

Serves 2   Cooking Time: 3-4 Minutes

INGREDIENTS

½ cup oats*
½ cup cornflakes
½ cup curd
1 boiled potato - finely chopped
¾ cup boiled kabuli channa (white bengal gram) or kaala channas (black gram)
1 green chilli - chopped
2 tbsp green coriander (hara dhania) - chopped
1 tomato - chopped finely
¼ tsp each salt or kala namak & red chilli powder
¼ tsp bhuna jeera powder

MITHI CHUTNEY
1 tbsp amchoor, 2 tbsp sugar, ¼ cup water
½ tsp salt, ½ tsp red chilli powder &
½ tsp bhuna jeera (roasted cumin powder)

METHOD

1. For mithi chutney, mix all ingredients. Cook for a few minutes, stirring continuously, till slightly thick. Remove from fire and keep aside.

2. Roast 1 cup oats* in a kadhai for 5 minutes on medium flame. Remove from fire. Keep aside.

3. Beat curd with salt or kala namak and red chilli powder. Keep aside.

4. Mix potato, channa, chilli, chopped coriander, and tomato with chutney in a big bowl.

5. Just at the time of serving, add the oats* and the cornflakes and curd. Quickly mix lightly with two forks.

6. Sprinkle some bhuna jeera (roasted cumin) powder and fresh coriander.

7. Serve immediately otherwise it tends to become soggy.

* For best results, Nita Mehta recommends Quaker Oats.

Oat-Moong Toast

Pulse and oat batter, coated on bread and panfried. Serve it along with hari chutney.

Serves 2   Cooking Time: 3-4 Minutes

INGREDIENTS

½ cup oats* - roasted
¼ cup dhuli Moong dal - soaked for 1-2 hours
2 green chillies - chopped
½ cup coriander leaves - chopped finely
½ tsp baking powder
1½ tsp lemon juice
1¼ tsp salt or to taste
a pinch of red chilli powder
4-5 tbsp oil
4 slices bread

METHOD

1. Drain and grind dal along with green chillies to a fine paste.

2. Mix moong dal paste, oats*, coriander leaves, baking powder, lemon juice, salt and red chilli powder. Add water to make a paste.

3. Heat 4-5 tbsp oil in a non stick pan.

4. Spread the oat mixture on one side of the bread slice with a spoon.

5. Invert the slice with the oat paste down in the hot oil.

6. Spread some oat paste on the upper side of the slice too, with a spoon. Turn. Shallow fry on both sides until light brown.

7. Remove from pan on to a paper napkin to absorb any excess oil.

8. Cut into two triangles.

9. Serve hot with tomato sauce or mint chutney.

* For best results, Nita Mehta recommends Quaker Oats.

Oat Hearts

Heart shaped small cutlets. Enjoy them with tomato ketchup.

Serves 2 Cooking Time: 4-5 Minutes

INGREDIENTS

1½ cup oats*
2 potatoes - boiled and mashed
¼ cup grated paneer
1 tsp salt or to taste
½ tsp red chilli powder
¼ tsp garam masala
½ tsp amchoor
2 tbsp chopped coriander
2 tbsp grated carrot
¼ tsp lemon juice

METHOD

1. Keep ½ cup oats* aside for coating

2. Mix all the other ingredients with 1 cup oats*.

3. Make 8-10 balls of the above mixture.

4. Flatten each ball and shape into hearts or cut with a heart shape cookie cutter. Do not flatten too much.

5. Spread the remaining ½ cup oats* on a plate. Dip each heart in a bowl of water for a second and immediately press both sides of each heart in oats*. Press hearts with the palms to make the oats* coat properly.

6. To pan fry the hearts, heat 1-2 tbsp oil in a pan. Fry 3-4 hearts at a time. When the underside turns golden, turn. Fry this side for a few minutes. Remove. Add more pieces. Serve with toasted slices.

* For best results, Nita Mehta recommends Quaker Oats.

Hari Chutney

Mint & coriander, a great combination for a relish. This green relish goes very well with Indian snacks.

Serves 6   Cooking Time: 2 Minutes

INGREDIENTS

¼ cup poodina leaves (½ bunch)
1 cup hara dhania (coriander) - chopped along with the stem
2 green chillies - chopped
1-2 flakes garlic - chopped finely (½ tsp)
1 onion - chopped
1 tbsp lemon juice, or to taste
1½ tsp sugar, ½ tsp salt, a pinch of black salt

METHOD

1. Wash coriander and mint leaves.
2. Grind all ingredients with just enough water to get the right chutney consistency.

Mithi Saunth

Made from raw mango powder, this sweet & sour chutney is a hit!

Serves 4   Cooking Time: 3-4 Minutes

INGREDIENTS

2 tbsp amchoor
4 tbsp sugar
½ tsp salt
¼ tsp red chilli powder
½ tsp roasted jeera powder
½ cup water

METHOD

1. Mix all the ingredients in a pan. Boil.
2. Cook for few minutes, stirring continuously till slightly thick. Remove from fire.

* For best results, Nita Mehta recommends Quaker Oats.

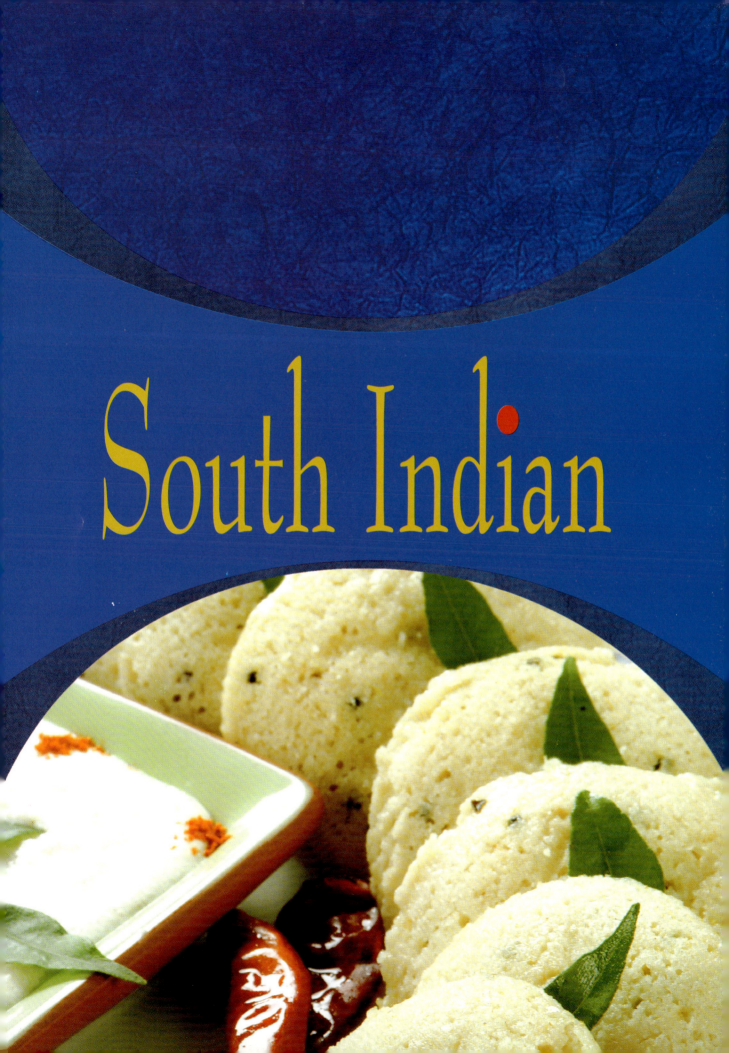
South Indian

Oat Pea Dosa

Rice has been replaced completely by oats*. A much healthier option. Serve it with chutney.

Makes 5 dosas   Cooking Time: 4-5 Minutes

INGREDIENTS

1 cup oats*
¼ cup dhuli urad dal or ¼ cup urad dal powder
1½ cups water (approx.)
½ tsp salt
oil for shallow frying

FILLING
1 tbsp oil
2 cups boiled peas
½ tsp rai (brown mustard seeds)
½ tsp salt and red chilli powder, or to taste

METHOD

1. For the filling, heat oil in a pan. Put rai and when it crackles, add salt, red chilli powder and peas. Stir fry for 2-3 minutes. Keep the filling aside.

2. Grind oats* and urad dal separately in a mixer to a powder. You can use readymade urad dal powder too.

3. Combine oats* powder, dal powder and salt. Put enough water to make a batter of thin pouring consistency.

4. Heat a pan. Put oil and wipe it off. Remove from fire. Take a ladle full of batter and spread from inside to outside.

5. Return to fire. When the edges turn brown, put a few drops of oil on the sides and on the dosa.

6. Put some filling. Fold over. Serve with oat chutney.

Note: Don't keep the batter for too long as it becomes more and more thick.

* For best results, Nita Mehta recommends Quaker Oats.

Corn Oat Upma

The South Indian breakfast made with oats*. Enjoy it with a good cup of coffee.

Serves 2-3 — Cooking Time: 10-12 Minutes

INGREDIENTS

1 cup oats* - powdered in a mixer
½ tsp sarson (mustard seeds)
1 dry red chilli (sookhi lal mirch)
2 tbsp channe ki dal (split gram)
1 tsp urad dhuli dal (split black beans)
10-12 curry leaves - optional
1 onion - chopped finely
1 tomato - chopped
2 cups water
1½ tsp salt
½ cup corn kernels - boiled or frozen
½ capsicum - chopped finely
juice of 1 lemon
4 tbsp oil

METHOD

1. In a clean heavy bottomed kadhai, heat 4 tbsp oil. Reduce heat. Add sarson.

2. Remove from fire. Add the dry red chilli, channa and urad dal and curry leaves. Stir till dal turns light brown.

3. Return to fire. Add onions. Fry till onions turn golden brown.

4. Add water and salt. Let it come to a boil.

5. Cover & cook on low flame for 3-4 minutes till the dal is cooked and is no longer crunchy.

6. Keeping the flame low, add chopped tomato and corn kernels. Stir.

7. Add oats* gradually with one hand, stirring with the other hand continuously.

8. Stir fry the upma for 3-4 minutes till dry. Turn off the fire and add capsicum and lemon juice. Mix well.

9. To serve, transfer some hot upma in a steel katori. Press lightly. Place the serving plate on the katori and holding the katori in one hand and pressing the plate with the other hand, invert the katori on to the plate to get a heap of upma for an individual serving.

* For best results, Nita Mehta recommends Quaker Oats.

Crunchy Oat Poha

Forget the rice flakes! Oats* are definitely healthier for the family.

Serves 4-5   Cooking Time: 5-6 Minutes

INGREDIENTS

2 cups oats*
1 potato - boiled & cut into small cubes
1 cup boiled peas (matar)
5 tbsp oil
½ tsp sarson (mustard seeds)
1 sprig of curry leaves - optional
½ tsp haldi (turmeric powder)
1 tsp salt, or to taste
½ tsp red chilli powder
1 green chilli - chopped finely
2 tbsp chopped coriander (optional)
juice of ½ lemon, or to taste
a pinch of sugar

METHOD

1. Roast oats* in a kadhai for 2-3 minutes. Keep aside.

2. Boil a potato and cut it into small cubes.

3. Heat oil. Add sarson. Reduce heat. Wait for 30 seconds. Add curry leaves.

4. Add haldi, salt and red chilli powder. Stir.

5. Add potatoes, peas and green chilli. Cook for a few seconds on medium heat.

6. Add oats*. Cook with occasional stirring for a few minutes.

7. Stir carefully so that the grains remain separate and unbroken. Remove from fire. Add lemon juice and sugar. Mix.

8. Serve garnished with chopped coriander leaves.

* For best results, Nita Mehta recommends Quaker Oats.

Mini Vegetable Oat Oothapam

These thick South Indian pancakes can be prepared without having to wait for the batter to ferment. The sour yogurt and eno take care of the lightness without fermentation.

Serves 2-3   Cooking Time: 3-4 Minutes

INGREDIENTS

BATTER
½ cups oats* - ground in a mixer to a powder
¾ cup sour yogurt (khatti dahi)
1 tsp salt
¼ tsp hing (asafoetida powder)
¼ tsp eno fruit salt

TOPPING
½ cup grated paneer
1-2 green chillies - chopped
a few curry leaves - chopped
1 onion - chopped, 1 tomato - chopped
¼ cup peas - boiled, ¼ cup cabbage - chopped
¼ tsp black pepper powder
salt to taste

METHOD

1. Except eno mix all ingredients of the batter together.

2. Add enough water (½ cup approx.) to the batter to get a thick pouring consistency. Beat well.

3. Keep the batter aside for ½ hour.

4. At the time of preparing oothapam, add eno and mix well.

5. Mix all ingredients of the topping together. Keep aside.

6. Heat a non stick tawa. Put 1 tbsp of oil on it and then wipe with a potato or onion cut into half.

7. Mix the batter well. Keeping the gas on low flame, pour 1 small karchhi (2 tbsp) of batter on it. Spread the batter a little with the back of the karchhi, keeping it slightly thick. Make 3-4 small rounds on the tawa.

8. Sprinkle a little topping on each and pour 2 tsp oil on the sides. Press the topping a little with a potato masher or spoon. Keep on low heat for a few seconds.

9. After the edges turn golden and the underside is cooked, turn the side carefully.

10. Remove from tawa after the other side also gets cooked and the onions turn a little brown.

11. Serve hot with coconut chutney or tomato ketchup.

* For best results, Nita Mehta recommends Quaker Oats.

Oat Vada

Oats* add a wonderful crunch to vadas.

Serves 2-3 Cooking Time: 4-5 Minutes

INGREDIENTS

¾ cup oats*
¼ cup chana dal (bengal gram split)
1 onion - chopped
½ tsp salt
a pinch of red chilli powder
1 green chilli - chopped
1 tbsp coriander - chopped
½ cup milk, approx.
oil for frying

METHOD

1. Soak chana dal for ½ an hour in hot water. Drain water and grind coarsely in a mixer.

2. Mix dal, oats*, chopped onion, salt, red chilli powder, green chilli, coriander and milk together. Mash it well. Add enough milk to get a soft paste.

3. Heat oil in a pan. Divide the mixture into 8 equal balls. Before making vadas apply little water on your hands to avoid sticking of the mixture.

4. Flatten the balls and deep fry on medium flame till golden brown.

* For best results, Nita Mehta recommends Quaker Oats.

Dakshini Toast with Oats

Continental snack with a South Indian touch.

Serves 2   Cooking Time: 4-5 Minutes

INGREDIENTS

2 tbsp oats* - powdered in a mixer
½ cup oats*
½ cup paneer - crumbled
½ tsp salt, or to taste
¼ tsp pepper, or to taste
½ onion - very finely chopped
2 tbsp curry leaves - chopped
½ tomato - cut into half, deseeded and chopped finely
4 bread slices
½ tsp rai (small brown mustard seeds)
3 tsp oil to shallow fry

METHOD

1. Mix ½ cup oats*, salt and pepper with the paneer lightly with your fingers.

2. Add the onion, tomato and curry leaves.

3. Spread paneer mixture carefully on bread slices, keeping edges neat.

4. Sprinkle some rai and powdered oats* over the paneer mixture, pressing down gently with finger tips.

5. Heat 1 tsp oil in a non stick pan. Add a slice of bread with topping side down.

6. Cook until the topping turns golden brown and crisp. Turn and cook from the other side. Add a little more oil for the next slice. Cut each slice into 2 pieces and serve hot with tomato ketchup.

Note: This recipe will work best using a minimum quantity of oil for frying.

* For best results, Nita Mehta recommends Quaker Oats.

Oat Idli

Half of the suji has been replaced by oat powder making the idli much lighter and more nutritious.

Makes 3   Cooking Time: 20 minutes

INGREDIENTS

½ cup oats* - grind to a powder
½ cup suji (semolina)
1 cup yogurt
½ cup water, approx.
¾ tsp eno fruit salt
¼ tsp salt
oil for greasing

METHOD

1. Grind oats* in a mixer to a powder. Put oat powder, suji, yogurt & salt in a bowl. Beat well.

2. Add enough water (about ½ cup) to make a smooth batter of thick, yet slightly pouring consistency. Keep the idli batter aside for 15-20 minutes.

3. Boil 2 cups of water in a cooker or a large pan (patila). Grease idli stand.

4. Now add eno to the idli batter. Mix well.

5. Put 2 tbsp of batter in each idli cup.

6. Place the idli stand in boiling water and cover the pan with a tight lid. If using a pressure cooker then remove weight from the lid.

7. Steam for 15 minutes on medium flame and check with a knife in the center. If it comes out clean, it is done take out and serve with oat chutney.

* For best results, Nita Mehta recommends Quaker Oats.

Oat Coconut Chutney

Although coconut has been used, still the use of oat powder has reduced the high calorie coconut.

Makes 1 cup   Cooking Time: 2-3 Minutes

INGREDIENTS

¼ cup oats*
½ cup grated coconut
½ cup yogurt
½ green chilli chopped
¼ tsp salt

TEMPERING
½ tsp oil
½ tsp mustard seeds
2 whole red chillies - broken into pieces
few curry leaves

METHOD

1. Scrape the brown skin of the coconut and grate it.

2. Grind oats* in a mixer to make powder.

3. Add yogurt, grated coconut, chopped green chilli and salt in the above oats* powder. Churn all the ingredients together to get a smooth paste. Keep aside in a bowl.

4. Heat oil. Put mustard seeds. When they starts cracking add broken whole red chillies and curry leaves. Remove from fire.

5. Add this tempering to chutney. Serve with dosa, idli or any South Indian snack.

* For best results, Nita Mehta recommends Quaker Oats.

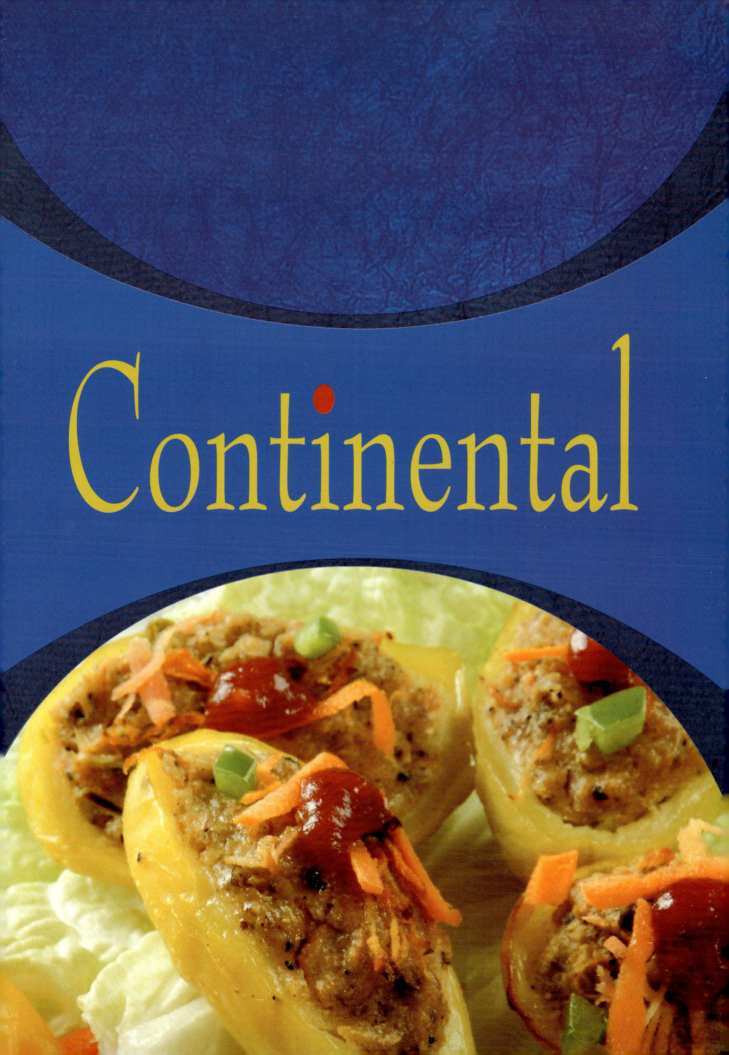

Oat Patty Sandwiches

If you are short of time in the mornings, prepare the patty (tikki) the previous evening and refrigerate. Use slices of brown bread or buns if available.

Serves 4   Cooking Time: 6-7 Minutes

INGREDIENTS

PATTY (TIKKI)
1½ cup oats*
4 potatoes - boiled & grated
1 onion - finely chopped, 2 tbsp oil
1 carrot - grated
10-12 french beans - chopped or 1 capsicum - chopped
1½ tsp salt or to taste, ½ tsp oregano
½ tsp pepper, ½ tsp red chilli flakes or powder

OTHER INGREDIENTS
5-6 tbsp thick curd
3 fresh burger buns or bread slices, preferably brown
a few lettuce or cabbage leaves - remove hard stem and tear into 1" pieces
a few tomato slices

METHOD

1. For the patty (tikki), heat 2 tbsp oil, add onion, cook till onion turns golden.

2. Add 1 cup oats*. Cook for 1 minute. Keep the remaining ½ cup oats* aside.

3. Add carrots and beans or capsicum, cook for 2-3 minutes.

4. Add salt, oregano, pepper and red chilli flakes. Cook for 2-3 minutes. Add boiled and grated potatoes. Cook for 5 minutes. Remove from fire. Check seasonings. Make balls and shape into round patties (tikki).

5. Spread the remaining ½ cup oats* in a plate.

6. Take a flat bowl with some water, dip the tikki in water for a second to wet it and then immediately press on ½ cup oats* spread in a plate. Turn sides to coat tikki properly. Keep in the fridge to chill for 10 minutes.

7. To assemble, shallow fry tikkis in 2-3 tbsp oil in a non stick pan, till brown and crisp. Keep aside.

8. Cut the buns into half, saute in a little oil or butter in the pan. Keep pressing the bread or buns lightly till soft. Remove from pan.

9. To assemble, spread curd on a bun, place a few pieces of cabbage or lettuce leaves. Place a hot tikki on it and then spread some curd. Arrange a slice of tomato. Sprinkle a pinch of salt & pepper, dot with a tsp curd and serve hot.

* For best results, Nita Mehta recommends Quaker Oats.

Spanish Oat Omelette

The addition of oats* to omelette keeps the cholesterol in check.

Makes 2 Omelettes   Cooking Time 4-5 Minutes

INGREDIENTS

1 cup oats*
4 eggs
1 tsp salt
½ tsp pepper
2 tbsp milk
1 small capsicum - finely sliced
1 small onion - finely sliced
½ small tomato - finely sliced
2 mushrooms - finely sliced (optional)
1 tbsp butter or oil

METHOD

1. Beat the eggs, oats*, salt, pepper and milk.

2. Heat butter or oil in a nonstick pan, keeping the flame low. Pour half of the egg mixture and roll the pan to cover the bottom.

3. Sprinkle capsicum, onion, tomato, mushrooms on top and press gently and cover the pan.

4. Cook for 1-2 minutes on low heat till the vegetables get steamed. Turn the side and cook well until light golden. Make the other omelette with the remaining egg mixture.

5. Serve with vegetable side up. Cut into wedges, serve hot with toasted bread.

* For best results, Nita Mehta recommends Quaker Oats.

Oat Mushroom Croquettes

Enjoy these rolls with buttered toasts for a complete breakfast.

Serves 2-3   Cooking Time: 20 Minutes

INGREDIENTS

½ cup oats*
2 tbsp butter
1 onion - chopped
¼ cup chopped mushrooms
¾ cup milk, approx.
salt & pepper to taste
3-4 tbsp green coriander - chopped
2 green chillies - chopped

METHOD

1. Heat 2 tbsp butter. Add onion. Saute till light pink.

2. Add the chopped mushroom. Saute for 2 minutes. Add oats*. Mix.

3. Add milk stirring continuously with the other hand. Cook till it turns thick and starts leaving the sides of the pan. Add salt and pepper. Remove from fire. Keep aside.

4. Add coriander and chillies. Mix well and cool the mixture. It can also be refrigerated for a while.

5. Shape the mixture into 7-8 croquettes (oblong rolls with flat sides).

6. Brush them from top with some melted butter.

7. Grill in the oven for 10-15 minutes. Turn side once after 5 minutes. Serve hot with ketchup and toasts.

Note: If you like, pan fry in 2 tbsp oil.

* For best results, Nita Mehta recommends Quaker Oats.

Fruit Medley Topped with Crunchy Oats

Delicious, light and healthy! Although the name suggests only fruit, it also has vegetables like cucumber, tomato and yam (kachaalu). Yam (kachaalu) is a vegetable which looks like a potato but has a taste similar to colocasia (arbi).

Serves 2-3   Cooking Time: 8 Minutes

INGREDIENTS

½-¾ cup oats* - roasted
2 cups papaya (papita) - cut into 1" pieces
1 apple - cut into ½" pieces with the peel
½ cup green or black grapes (angoor)
½ cup of cucumber (kheera) - cut into ½" pieces with the peel
½ tomato - cut into thin long pieces
½ banana (kela) - cut into round slices
½ kachaalu (yam) - boiled, optional or 1 kiwi
1 tbsp very finely chopped coriander, optional

OTHER INGREDIENTS
3½ tsp ready-made chat masala
1 tsp bhuna jeera powder (roasted cumin powder)
2 tbsp powdered sugar
juice of 1½ large lemons

METHOD

1. To boil kachaalu, put it in a pressure cooker. Cover with water. Pressure cook to give 1 whistle. Reduce heat and keep on low heat for 4-5 minutes. Remove from fire. Let it cool. Peel the kachalu and cut it into 4 pieces lengthwise. Cut each slice width wise into thin slices, to get small triangular slices.

2. Put it in a big bowl. Mix all vegetables and fruits in the bowl.

3. Sprinkle chat masala, bhuna jeera, powdered sugar. Squeeze lemon juice over it. Toss lightly with a fork. Taste and adjust spices.

4. At serving time mix roasted oats*. Serve with toothpicks or small snack forks.

Note: Any fruits like watermelon, oranges, kiwis, mangoes etc. can be added according to your choice and availability.

* For best results, Nita Mehta recommends Quaker Oats.

Oat Pretzels

These soft pretzels can be taken with jam & butter for breakfast. Makes a good snack with soup too.

Serves 4   Cooking Time: 15-20 Minutes

INGREDIENTS

1¼ cup oats* - powdered very finely in a mixer
1 cup flour (maida)
1 tsp salt
2 tsp dry yeast, ½ tsp sugar
slightly less than 1 cup (150 ml) warm water
15 gm (1 tbsp) salted butter

METHOD

1. Mix ¼ cup warm water with ½ tsp sugar. Dissolve yeast in it. Cover and keep aside in a warm place for 10 minutes to make it frothy. If the yeast does not turn frothy, discard. Start with a new pack of yeast. (see note)

2. Sieve flour, oat powder and salt. Mix in the frothy yeast mixture.

3. Knead to a soft smooth dough with warm water. Knead well for about 10 minutes.

4. Beat butter till creamy. Mix the whipped butter into the dough and knead well. Keep aside in a greased polythene in a warm place for 1 hour to swell.

5. Punch the dough down to it's original volume. Keep aside in a warm place for 45 minutes.

6. Divide into 8 portions. Shape them into long rolls like a 5-7" long thick rope. Tie the two ends of the rope to get a knotted pretzel.

7. Place on a greased tray covered with a cloth for 10 minutes.

8. Bake in a preheated oven at 450°F/230°C for 15-20 minutes till golden.

Note: Dry yeast does not get activated if it is more than 6-8 months old. Do check the date of manufacture before buying.

* For best results, Nita Mehta recommends Quaker Oats.

Quick Oat Sandwiches

Curd and oat mixture spread on bread and toasted till crisp.

Serves 2　　　　　　　　　　　　　　　　　　　　　　　　　　Cooking Time: 3-4 Minutes

INGREDIENTS

½ cup oats* - roasted
4 slices bread - buttered lightly
½ cup curd - beat well till smooth
1 tbsp chopped capsicum
2 tbsp grated carrots
a pinch of bhuna jeera
salt and pepper, to taste
1 tsp tomato ketchup

METHOD

1. Dry roast oats* in a kadhai for 3-4 minutes till light brown or fragrant.

2. Mix whipped curd, ketchup, roasted oats*, chopped capsicum, carrots, salt, pepper and jeera.

3. Spread 2 heaped tbsp of the above mixture on one side of a bread slice.

4. Cover with another slice.

5. Toast the sandwich on a non-stick pan on both sides till golden. Cut into two. Serve.

* For best results, Nita Mehta recommends Quaker Oats.

Sesame Spinach Oat Toasts

Bread topped with spinach - oat mixture and grilled in the oven till crisp.

Serves 2   Cooking Time: 15 Minutes

INGREDIENTS

½ cup oats*
4 brown bread slices
1 cup finely chopped spinach (paalak) leaves
1 small onion - chopped
1½ tbsp butter
salt, pepper to taste, ½ cup milk
4 tsp tomato ketchup
2 tsp sesame seeds
a few tomato slices - cut into strips for garnishing

METHOD

1. Heat 1½ tbsp butter. Add oats*, cook for 3- 4 minutes.

2. Add the chopped onion. Saute for a minute.

3. Add the chopped spinach. Saute for 2 minutes. Add salt and pepper. Mix.

4. Add milk stirring continuously with the other hand. Cook for 1-2 minutes. Remove from fire. Keep aside.

5. Spread 1 tsp tomato ketchup on each slice.

6. Spread some spinach mixture on it. Sprinkle sesame seeds.

7. Garnish with tomato strips.

8. Bake in a preheated oven at 200°C for 3-4 minutes or more till the bread gets toasted. Cut into 2 triangles or serve whole.

* For best results, Nita Mehta recommends Quaker Oats.

Oat Club Sandwiches

3 layered sandwiches with a vegetable and oat spread. You can take it plain or grill them for a toasted flavour.

Serves 2
Cooking Time: 8-10 Minutes

INGREDIENTS

6 slices bread
50 gms paneer (cottage cheese) - cut into thin slices
1 tbsp tomato ketchup
8 round slices of cucumber (kheera)

MIX TOGETHER
¼ cup roasted oats*
2 tbsp grated carrot (gajar)
2 tbsp shredded cabbage (bandgobhi)
¼ cup curd
¼ tsp oregano
salt, pepper to taste

METHOD

1. Heat ½ tsp butter on a non stick tawa. Add the paneer slices. Saute for 1-2 minutes till brown patches appear on the underside. Turn the paneer slices. Shut off the fire.

2. Take a slice of bread. Apply little ketchup and spread the oats* and vegetable mixture on it. Place one paneer slice over it. Sprinkle salt and pepper.

3. Take a slice and spread little ketchup and oats* mixture on both the sides.

4. Invert this slice over the paneer slice.

5. Place cucumber slices over the bread slice and sprinkle some salt and pepper.

6. Apply oats* mixture on the inner side of the third slice.

7. Invert this third slice over the cucumber slices. Press. Grill for 3-4 minutes. Cut the edges of the bread.

8. Cut into two triangles and serve immediately.

9. Repeat with the other three slices.

* For best results, Nita Mehta recommends Quaker Oats.

Oat Potato Shells

Who say potatoes are unhealthy & fattening! Yes, they are if you fry them. Here we have stuffed them with a delicious oat filling and grilled them to perfection.

Serves 4   Cooking Time: 20-25 Minutes

INGREDIENTS

½ cup oats*
½ cup curd
2 tbsp grated carrot
½ tsp salt
¼ tsp black pepper
4 potatoes - boiled
1 tbsp chopped mint leaves
1 tbsp melted butter

METHOD

1. Mix oats*, curd, grated carrot, salt & pepper. Keep aside.

2. Cut the boiled potato lengthwise. Scoop it with a peeler, leaving ¼" wall all around.

3. Brush the walls and the outside of the potatoes with melted butter.

4. Fill the oat* mixture in the scooped potato and top with some chopped mint leaves.

5. Cover the wire rack with aluminium foil and grease with oil.

6. Place potato shells on the greased foil and bake at 180°C for 20 minutes. Serve hot.

* For best results, Nita Mehta recommends Quaker Oats.

Mayonnaise (Eggless)

Goes well with sandwiches, chips, rolls, cutlets or any other snack.

INGREDIENTS

3 tbsp oil, 2 tbsp flour (maida)
½ cup cold milk, 1 tsp lemon juice
50 gm (¼ cup) cream, ½ tsp mustard powder
1 tsp powdered sugar, ¼ tsp salt
¼ tsp pepper powder

METHOD

1. Heat oil in a small heavy bottomed pan. Add flour. Reduce flame and stir for a minute. Add milk, stirring continuously. Boil. Cook till a thick white sauce is ready.

2. Whip white sauce after it cools to room temperature. Add lemon juice, salt, mustard powder, pepper and sugar.

3. Gently mix in cream. Keep in the fridge till serving time.

Chocolate Sauce

A squeeze of chocolate sauce on a dollop of ice cream or a piece of cake, transforms it. Makes it more interesting and delicious to eat.

Serves 4

INGREDIENTS

1 cup water
3 tsp cornflour
4 tbsp sugar
3 tbsp cocoa
2 tsp butter

METHOD

1. Mix all the above ingredients.

2. Cook on slow fire for 3-4 minutes, stirring continuously, till the sauce becomes thick and glossy.

3. It should coat the back of the spoon.

4. Serve over vanilla or chocolate ice creams.

* For best results, Nita Mehta recommends Quaker Oats.

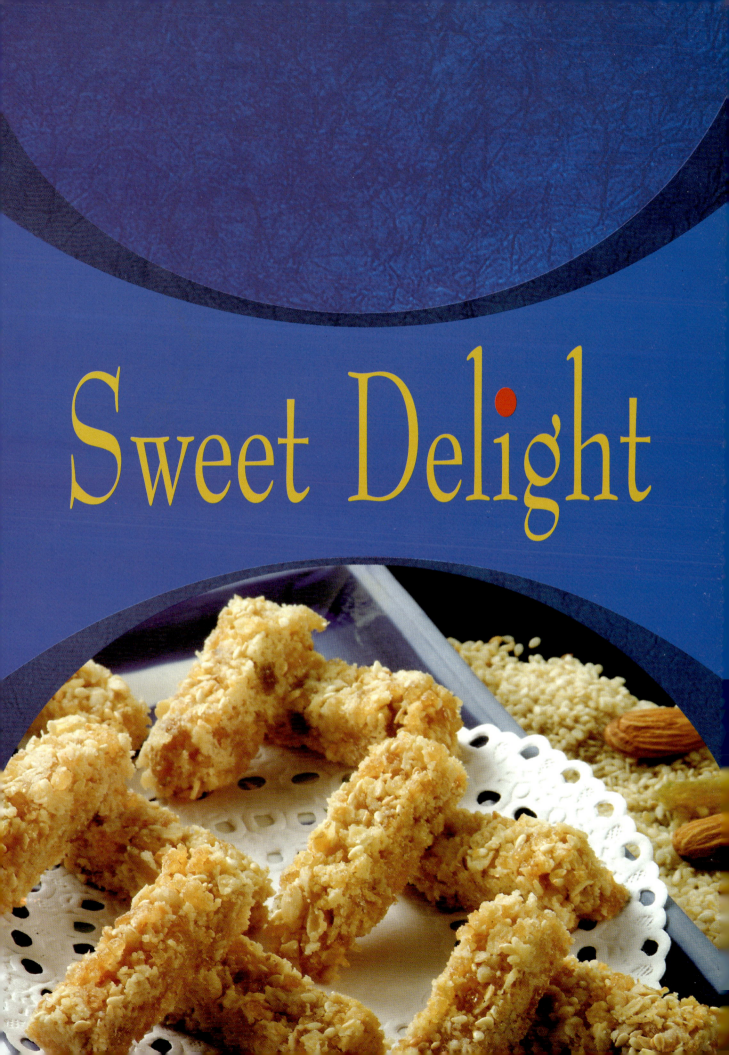

Oat Ka Halwa

A very healthy sweet treat for the growing children. A good change from the regular suji ka halwa.

Serves 2-3   Cooking Time: 8-10 Minutes

INGREDIENTS

1 cup oats* - powdered
6 tsp of desi ghee (clarified butter)
½ cup sugar
2 cups water
2 chhoti illaichi (green cardamom) - skinned and crushed
8-10 kishmish (raisins)
8-10 almonds (badam) - cut into thin long pieces

METHOD

1. Mix water, kishmish, crushed illaichi and sugar. Boil. Remove from fire. Stir to dissolve the sugar. Keep aside.

2. Heat ghee in a kadhai. Fry oats* on low heat till they just change colour.

3. Add sugar water mixture, stirring continuously for 3-4 minutes till the halwa leaves the sides of the kadhai. Remove from fire.

4. Keep in a serving dish. Decorate with shredded almonds. Serve hot.

* For best results, Nita Mehta recommends Quaker Oats.

Oat Fudge Fingers

Mixture of oats*, sesame seeds and raisins, all baked together and then cut into fingers.

Makes about 20 fingers

Cooking Time: 15-20 Minutes

INGREDIENTS

¾ cup oats*
¼ cup sesame seeds (til)
¾ cup brown sugar
2 tbsp raisins (kishmish)
¾ cup desiccated coconut (coconut powder)
½ cup melted white butter

METHOD

1. Mix oats*, sesame seeds, brown sugar, raisins and coconut.

2. Add melted butter. Mix well.

3. Take a small rectangular dish, or a square baking tin or an aluminium ice tray and place a sheet of aluminium foil in it. Grease the foil with oil. Now spread the mixture on the aluminium foil to get a ½" thick layer.

4. Bake in a preheated oven at 150°C for about 15 minutes till light golden. Remove from oven.

5. Cool to room temperature. Then keep in the refrigerator for 1 hour. Cut into fingers with a sharp knife.

Note: In winters there is no need to keep the mixture in the refrigerator before cutting.

* For best results, Nita Mehta recommends Quaker Oats.

Oat Coated Apples

Crunchy & delicious! Apple slices are rolled into oats* and baked.

Serves 2-3 Cooking Time: 10 Minutes

INGREDIENTS

1 cup oats*
2 apples - cut into 2" thick slices
¼ cup sugar
¼ cup water
1 tsp coffee
¼ tsp cinnamon (dalchini)

METHOD

1. Cut apples into thick slices without peeling.

2. Mix sugar, water, coffee & cinnamon powder in a pan. Bring to a boil. Simmer for 1 minute. Remove from fire.

3. Immediately dip the apples on both sides in the sugar syrup.

4. Coat all sides of the apple with the oats* spread in a plate.

5. Bake at 180° C for 10 minutes. Serve with honey.

* For best results, Nita Mehta recommends Quaker Oats.

Banana/Mango Oat Pancakes

Sweet & fruity! Healthy pancakes make for a delicious breakfast.

Makes 6 Cooking Time: 3-4 Minutes

INGREDIENTS

¾ cup oat powder
1 banana or 1 ripe mango - sliced
¼ cup maida (plain flour)
1 egg
½ - ¾ cup milk (approx.)
1 tsp sugar
1 tsp vanilla essence
oil for frying

METHOD

1. Grind sliced banana or sliced mango with a little milk in a mixer to get a puree.

2. Add oat powder, maida, egg, sugar, vanilla essence and remaining milk in the above banana puree. Mix well to get a batter of pouring consistency.

3. Heat a pan. Add a tsp of oil in the pan and spread it.

4. Add 2 tbsp of the pancake batter and spread it like a dosa. Return to fire. Put 1 tsp of oil around it. Remove from fire. Cover the pan with a lid. Leave for 2 minutes on medium flame.

5. Uncover, increase flame, put ½ tsp oil over the pancake & turn it. Let it cook for 1 minute.

6. Take it out on a plate and spread with jam or honey. Roll up and serve.

* For best results, Nita Mehta recommends Quaker Oats.

Apple Oat Cake

A very healthy cake. Whole wheat flour and apples combine with oats*!

Serves 10-12   Cooking Time: 40-45 Minutes

INGREDIENTS

1 cup oats* - grind to a powder in a mixer
¾ cup wheat flour (atta)
2 tsp cinnamon powder
2 tsp baking powder
1 tsp soda-bi-carb (mitha soda)
5 tbsp softened batter
1 cup powdered sugar
4 egg whites
½ - ¾ cup (approx.) milk
1 tsp vanilla essence
2 apples - peeled, cored and chopped (3 cups)

TOPPING
¼ cup brown sugar
1 tbsp oats*
1 tbsp wheat flour
1 tsp cinnamon powder

METHOD

1. Mix all the ingredients of topping together in a bowl. Keep aside.

2. Sieve wheat flour, cinnamon powder, baking powder and soda-bi-carb together.

3. Beat butter and sugar till creamy. Add egg whites and mix well.

4. Gradually add flour in it. Add ½ cup milk. Mix well.

5. Now put oat powder, vanilla essence and fold in 2 cups apples, keeping aside 1 cup for the top. If the mixture appears very thick, add some milk to get a soft dropping consistency.

6. Grease & dust a 9" round cake tin. Transfer the batter in it.

7. Spread 1 cup apples over the batter.

8. Sprinkle the topping all over the apples.

9. Bake in a pre-heated oven at 180°C for 40-45 minutes.

10. Remove from oven.

* For best results, Nita Mehta recommends Quaker Oats.